Self-Publishing:
An Insider's Guide

Self-Publishing: An Insider's Guide

Bill Hushion
&
Peter Wright

GUERILLA
Gourmet
CORP.

Any such inquiries should be directed to:

> Guerilla Gourmet Corp
> 2490 Oak Row Cres
> Mississauga, ON L5l 1P4
> 905-828-9888/866-261-4441

Ordering information:

> White Knight Book Distribution Services Ltd.
> Georgetown Terminal Warehouse
> 34 Armstrong Avenue
> Georgetown, Ontario L7G 4R9
> Phone: 905-873-2750
> Fax: 905-873-6170

Library and Archives Canada Cataloguing in Publication

Wright, Peter, 1956–
 Self-publishing : an insider's guide / Peter Wright, Bill Hushion.

Includes index.
ISBN 978-0-9689462-4-4

 1. Self-publishing. I. Hushion, Bill, 1940– II. Title.

Z285.5.H88 2007   070.5'93   C2007-904586-3

Design: Fortunato Design Inc.
Cover illustration: Karen Petherick
Printer: Transcontinental Printing

Printed in Canada

Table of Contents

Preface

I'M GOING TO MAKE YOU 2 PROMISES: 1, in the time it will take you to read this—60 minutes or so—you will know enough about self-publishing to allow you, should you so choose, to bring your book to market, and 2, you will know the right way to do it. If you give Bill Hushion, my coauthor, who was a senior vice president of a major publishing company and then a distributor for many years, an opportunity to discuss if there's a wrong way to self-publish, make sure you're sitting far enough back since he tends to become quite passionate on this subject. Why? He's seen too many people spend far too much money and paint themselves into a corner by making well-meaning error after well-meaning error.

Why is someone with this depth of experience's opinion valuable? Simply put, as a distributor, he would be responsible to sell your book to major bookstores that won't deal with single title publishers. He's the kind of person you'd pay to be in front of. I, on the other hand, am the one who will throw a healthy dose of realism on your parade. Why? Because the main problem with this book industry, in my opinion, is that there's no guaranteed formula for success— either for established or us self-published authors. You can do all the right things and still end up with a basement full of books. You can do some of the right things by accident and end up with a book that sells.

So, that's the aim with this book, to give you an insider's view of how to do things right—which still won't guarantee success, it will merely guarantee you keep more of your money in the pocket where it belongs. There's a process to the self-publishing book business and you're going to learn it over the next hour. You can argue, disagree and believe you and your book will be the exception, but you will probably be wrong. And "wrong," in the self-publishing world, is another word for "will cost you more money."

So, sit back, have a pen handy and think of the questions you'd like to ask a bona fide distributor, which, by the way, will be the most important singular element of this exercise. The beauty of having a distributor's perspective early in the game, for those of you who took Marketing 101, is they have an eye on what sells, as they're the ones on the front lines. They're the ones speaking to book buyers, so if they make suggestions on your book cover or the size of font or the dearth or saturation of images in your book, it's best to listen. Students of Marketing know it's a little more prudent to try to make something the market wants than make something because it can be made.

Introduction:
If you do it, do it right

I F INDEED YOU DO SELF-PUBLISH YOUR BOOK, you will be in
a growing category: 25% of all books being published in
North America today are self-published. It's also important
to realize some publishing industry people still think self-
publishing is a dirty word, a word that suggests a not-quite-
ready-for-primetime effort, but this is changing. Mind you,
I think the best advice anybody—anybody considerate, that
is—could ever give to someone considering writing and
publishing a book is... don't. Don't do it—unless you are
utterly driven to see it all the way through. Knowing the
concrete steps to a self-published book may be *proactive*, but
being prepared for the soul-dropping disappointment of
nobody showing up at your book signing is *protective*.

But, what if the self-publishing planets are in line and
you've stumbled upon a book for the ages—exactly when
people want to read it and the media want to talk about it?
What about if while you drive, you think of great book ideas,
winning book titles, exciting book marketing plans and you
can envision talk show hosts discussing your book on
NATIONAL TV!! Do you find yourself yearning to refer to
yourself as an author? You know, all too well, that writing a
book is among the 3 top personal goals people have, but so
few have the discipline to sit down and do it. I recently gave
a seminar on self-publishing to a community group, along
with the coauthor of this book and a representative from a
printing firm. Thirty-five people filled the small lecture hall,
each with earnest, enthusiastic and eager looks on their faces.
The seminar lasted for three hours. When it was over, I was

very proud of the information we had conveyed. I thought we had done a bang up job of condensing the 5 pillars of self-publishing—**writing/editing, designing, printing, distributing and promotion/publicity**—into a comprehensive, easy-to-follow seminar. We gave the facts—with no attempt to sugarcoat the necessary steps. Why am I bringing this up? I'm bringing this up because you'd have to have seen the looks on their faces to believe it. To see their faces go from eager and hopeful to all but crushed and defeated was fascinating. Why was it fascinating? No, it's not because I'm sadistic; it's more the realization that people were hoping the entire exercise would be easier and less expensive. When they realized how much time it takes to have a successful, well-distributed, self-published book, how many people will ultimately be involved and how much money is required to get it done properly, most of them seemed to mentally give up.

And that, my fellow writers, is the point. If a three hour seminar on self-publishing can quash your hopes, that was the best $44. ever spent. Why? Because the $44. saved them $10,000 and untold grief—if that's the way they saw it. And if your hopes can be quashed by some facts and perspective, then be happy if was before you spent your money and the better part of 2 years.

On the other hand, on a personal note, nothing I've done—except for being a parent to my two boys and daughter—compares to the pride and the satisfaction of being an author, and knowing that my writing has either improved someone's life or had an impact in some way. My first book was aimed at single dads, *Cook Like a Mother! Clean Like a Pro! The Single Dad's Guide to Cooking and Cleaning*, and recently I got an email from a guy in Wisconsin who had purchased my book. He went on to tell me he had purchased a few of the things I recommended in my book, like, a pressure cooker. The most significant thing for me was his description of how his kids liked his cooking better now, after reading my book. My second book, *Home Ec for the Domestically Challenged*, has helped many people overcome their fear (and loathing?) in the kitchen. That is what I'm talking about. If you believe in your heart that you can influence someone and help them through the death of a loved one, the start-up of a new company, help them buy real estate, choose a car, learn to hang glide, dance, buy a pet, have more sex, do more, do it better—whatever—then you will have the intestinal fortitude to see it through.

Bookstore Realities

MANY PEOPLE DREAM OF WRITING A BOOK, no question. But it's important to note that approximately 320 new books are published every **single working day in the US alone**. Every author wants to be on Oprah. Everyone wants a huge advance. Every author wants a New York Times review. But 178,000 new books come out each year in the US alone, with about the same number in the UK and 16,000 in Canada. Furthermore, bookstores can't bend over backwards to sell your book—they're in the real estate business: publishing companies buy where books end up in the stores. Nothing happens by accident in bookstores. You want to be close to where the traffic is? You want a display of just your books? You want to be part of a themed display? No problem, just get out your checkbook. You want your book to have a chance? See the chapter on publicity and marketing!

When my first book was published, I expected royal treatment. I mean, come on, I invested the time and the money, I created a masterpiece; my book will sell like hotcakes, so put someone on it. Make it look good, make sure it's the first book people see coming into the store. I was of the extremely naïve view that book placement was tied to how good the book was. The reality, of course, is every single store I visited had to go to the storeroom to find it, and the ones who did have it on the shelves had the book spine out, with all the other books, it seemed, cover out. Chain bookstores are like grocery stores, stocking over a 100,000 titles, with feature display space purchased by the publisher/distributor. In a grocery store, the products you see on the end aisles or at eye level, those within easy reach and that don't require a huge amount of hunting to find, are there because their manufacturer or distributor paid for their placement. The same thing for books: what you see and stumble over as you walk into bookstores is influenced purely by revenue. So, all the books that were well known were going to remain well known and the newcomers were going to stay... unknown.

At any rate, let's get going—we've got books to publish!

Types of Self-Publishing

WHEN MOST OF US THINK OF SELF-PUBLISHING, we're thinking on a fairly big scale: writing a bestseller—a book with a big audience in mind, creating a book with a cover that can compete on the shelves of international book stores and then promoting the hell out of it. There are, of course, less grandiose, far more accomplishable—and more potentially profitable—ways of getting your book to materialize. Your book-publishing goal may be to sell 200 books. In this case, you probably don't need to spend the money to professionally design the book; you can go to a readily available instant printer, not a dedicated book printer (your local copy store will do). You don't need an ISBN number if you only plan on printing 25 copies to sell to your immediate family or employees.

The only thing that's really worth mentioning is the need to avoid painting yourself into a corner. Meaning, you have to walk a fine line between being reasonable with expectations while not cutting out any potential avenues. Becoming a self-published author means you not only have to wear many hats, you need to know when to change them. For example, let's say you spend $2,000 printing your book (200 x $10. is not unreasonable) and you're so happy you think, damn, I'll bet the public would like this book and you contact a distributor and he/she says, damn, I'll bet the bookstores would like this book. All you have to do is fix the cover, fix the masthead (the page with all the key information on it), get an ISBN number and a barcode. And all that's going to cost you is *another* $2,000.

That's what I mean by painting yourself into a corner. Frankly, I think that's probably the most difficult thing to avoid doing. You're trying to be confident and realistic at the same time. Or, if you're fond of oxymorons: Bullish and introspective, Aggressive and thoughtful. There are untold millions of examples of people who have mortgaged their house to create a world-class book, only to find there wasn't a market for it—or, there was a market for it, but they didn't have the marketing resources or the publicity prowess to cultivate it. There are fewer people indeed who wish they had spent more money than they did on book design and printing, only to discover there was a hidden market for their book. If this indeed happens to you, don't forget you can do a reprint with a new cover, even an entire new design. It may cost more in the long run, but you didn't extend yourself over the abyss of uncertain book demand.

Let's get back to some other forms of self-publishing:

Family—Recently I met a woman whose *direct* family consisted of over 1,000 relatives scattered from Scotland to Nova Scotia to Arizona to Maine. Over the course of 4 years she had compiled a family history that included photos, accounts of arguments (both sides got their say), letters, and so on. She printed 1,000 books. Now, every time she travels to, or visits, family, she takes books to sell, the proceeds from which offset—and sometimes exceed—her travel costs. Soon she'll have to do a reprint!

Company—You may have started a company with 3 people that has grown to 1,000 and you feel every employee should have an understanding of your corporate philosophy or your beginnings, as an essential element to working there. Or, you may run a lawn-care company in an area that has a number of similar companies. The difference? You've written a book about your lawn care secrets or a humorous account of your most eccentric customers. My coauthor, Bill Hushion, told me about a woman who wrote a book about her dog-walking company. Although she intended it solely for her clients and clients' friends as a way of attracting new business, the book struck a chord with the general (dog-loving) population. Whatever the inclination, armed with your laptop and a good battery, you can devote a fair amount of your weekends to writing a book.

Private—You may run a sports club, say a karate club, with Junior, Intermediate and Adult classes. Say you've got 30 people per class and your classes turn over quite frequently. You need a manual of katas (moves) and a forum to explain why your particular approach to karate is unique. Ergo, you write a book. Again, go through the same criteria as above.

Self-Published Categories That Haven't Seen Much (Success)

ARE THERE CATEGORIES OF SELF-PUBLISHING that are the book equivalent of high-risk plays in sports like throwing out of your end zone in a close football game, or trying a second tennis serve as hard as your first in a deciding match? Are there certain categories you should be very leery of self-publishing? Unfortunately the answer is yes. While it's good—even necessary—to be passionate and sometimes aggressive about your work, here are some self-publishing categories that are historically low-percentage plays (meaning, they rarely work in large distribution):

Fiction—This genre is best let to the extremely big boys with extremely big marketing machines and money. Money drives fiction success, all things being equal. There are probably few things that live the 'build a better mousetrap' adage better than fiction. You may have written a terrific story with great characters, unbearable suspense, a gripping drama, but you need a machine to market it. Yes, there are the JK Rowlings that get discovered, but she didn't self-publish, and the marketing machine behind her would make the US army blush.

Poetry—Something as delicate and personal as poetry deserves a better, kinder fate, so know this going in: poetry rarely sells as a self-published category.

Biography—There are people who have accomplished far more than the average person, they may have started a chain of submarine sandwiches that everyone loves, they may have been a popular high school football coach of an unusually high number of kids that went on to play professionally... no, forget that last example, there may be a story in there that's inspirational that could lead to a Speakers career, something we'll discuss later. Stick with the sub millionaire who thinks his/her story is worth telling. Unless there is murder, mayhem, manipulation and/or mutilation, they should probably forget about it. Remember the story about the guy back in the '80's who started a gull-winged car company, ran into financial trouble and then ran into an FBI drug sting? It was in the news; it involved the fabled FBI and drugs. This is the sort of biography that would work. Of course, the higher up the interest scale you go, the more interest you'd probably get from a publishing company.

Family—You know how when you're sitting around your family cottage some Sunday afternoon and everyone's there, everyone's a couple of pints in, and your cousin starts talking about how your uncle used to make everyone laugh by slurping Spaghetti-O's through a straw? And the stories start and flow very heavily all afternoon. And then everyone agrees a family member has to write a book because such shenanigans would never be believed and are just too funny not to tell? Well, by all means write it; just don't expect to sell it beyond the family.

Regional—Anything with a strong regional flavor. It will sell well within that region, something that might be your goal. It might sell well with tourist organizations within your region, just be aware strong regional flavors tend to limit broad appeal.

Teen Fiction—There are very few examples of successes in this genre. And I know it's kind of counter-intuitive, because there are so many teens right now, but it has the same limitations as adult fiction: it takes a big machine to get it moving.

Computer Books—This is a tough genre to sell is because there is a major glut of computer books on the market.

Pets—Fido has been an integral part of your family for almost 15 years. During those years, SO many funny and poignant things have happened and you have so many funny photos you could create a great book, couldn't you? You could and perhaps you should, but don't hold out too much hope that anyone other than you, your relatives and some very close friends will read it let alone buy it.

Of course, there are exceptions to every rule: Marley and Me originated as a self-published book that has sold upwards of 300,000 books; again, know the odds.

Self-Published Categories That Have Seen Success

ENOUGH OF THE NEGATIVE STUFF, what about categories that historically can and do work:

Motivational—Generally written by someone who's in or getting into Motivational Speaking. This is a great sales tool to get speaking engagements and to sell while you're at the engagement. It's a great category also to put into bookstores of markets you'll be speaking at when you do your local media (see chapter on Publicity and Promotion). Bill tells me, for a Motivational speaker, having a book can virtually double the fees a speaker demands. While approaching a company to offer a seminar on "Why Good Typing Is So Rewarding", if a speaker can direct the company to the closest bookstore to find their book, it greatly enhances three things: one, their credibility, 2, their image, and 3, their dough.

Business—This category of books tends to do well, Generally, Sales is the biggest topic, for obvious reasons—all sales people go through ruts they desperately want out of and will look for help through any means possible—including books. There are approximately 1,500 business titles published every year. Approximately 60-70% of all business books are purchased in bookstores. The balance is special sales, direct mail, business magazine coupon offerings, etc. Per square foot, the best place to sell a business book is an airport bookstore.

Cooking—Ruts don't just happen to sales people, of course; everybody can get into a rut, especially people making the same meals over and over again. Cookbooks offer the illusion of instant change. There are over 2,000 new cookbooks published each year. Bookstores account for 70% of book sales in this category, followed by Costco/Price Club, Sam's Club, etc., that account for about 15%. It's interesting to note that cookbooks are the number one collectible book, as a recent statistic would suggest: the average American woman owns *17* cook books, and readers of this genre are constantly looking for new additions to their collection. Please note: more than 65% of all cookbooks and craft books are now published as trade paperback originals, not hardcover.

Crafts/Hobbies—Same thing. People need diversion from their hectic lives and ways to keep their kids occupied.

Health—This is one of the fastest growing genres as baby boomers slowly realize they're mortal. We have an insatiable need for knowing how we can combat fatigue, extra weight, etc. These fall into several categories: Mainstream (i.e., how to avoid getting cancer), one is the before book, another is the after book, and another is the reference book. How to survive. There are three types of health books: how to prevent a disease or condition, how to survive the disease or condition and understanding the disease or condition. There are traditional health books and alternative health books. A new trend is emerging that addresses a combination of traditional and alternative medicine.

New Age—In our crass, shallow, material and mostly superficial world, alternative perspectives attract considerable attention. People need meaning, and this category provides it. New Age books have become increasingly popular over the past 20 years, as North Americans embrace Eastern ways of thinking and traditions. There are many

New Age specialty bookstores. The number 1 wholesaler that serves this market is New Leaf in the US.

Parenting—This is a consistently strong category. As society evolves, so do different methods of dealing with child and parenting issues. Children are better read, more media savvy than ever before. And since we're not supposed to spank our kids any more, most people appreciate anything that could help them cope. Anyone who has ever experienced the anguish of doubt over parenting will understand how well this category does. Answers. We're just after answers—pretty well in every category. And if it's not answers we're after, we're after ideas, anything to give us a track to run on when it's apparent we're running out of the tracks we're on.

Self-help/Relationships—Apart from fiction, there are more books published in this category than ever before. It's a hot market as everybody is looking for a quick fix to his or her problems—be it seeking the confidence to seek a raise or the patience to deal with a teenager. All you have to do is turn on the TV set for 5 or 6 hours a day and you will see nothing other than quick fix solutions to daily troubles: Oprah, Dr. Phil, Montel, The View, Rikki Lake, Jerry Springer are just the nationally-syndicated offerings. If you get this category right, you could make a lot of money—not just from book sales, but also as an expert who needs to be quoted and interviewed. The important thing is to spot the trend while it's hot. Everybody wants to live longer, be happier, make more money, have more sex and get along better with the people in their lives. There are times when what we're experiencing is beyond our ability to both understand and cope, so we try many things in an attempt to get through dark moments.

Travel books—These books can be divided into 3 categories: summer, winter and armchair. Some are intended to serve as guides to the people traveling into the area you've written about, so it had better be precise or you'll have some irate readers; the armchair travel books can be a celebration of a certain area, complete with your experiences, for example.

Children 0-12—Some of the richest writers in the world are children's book writers. They didn't make a million on one book, but over the series of books they wrote. Children's books are broken down into these categories. A children's book with less than 14 pages is not considered a children's book. It's a pamphlet.

Children's' books should be a minimum of 32 pages. They are divided into various age groups: 1-4, 4-8, 8-12, 12 and up. Each of these age groups categories represents the reading level that child has achieved.

Ages 1-4—Board books, very simple concept books, and numbers and shapes books. These books can be as little as 8 pages as in the case of a board book.

Ages 4-8—At least 80% of books in this category are picture books, 4 color, with a story line. It's important to get the reading level right on these books, as in make sure librarians, school teachers, and so on, check to make sure.

Ages 8-12—This category can have a combination of picture and words. Again, make sure you have someone check the language.

Ages 12 and up—Very difficult category. The most successful books in this category are series titles, with a minimum of two to six titles a year being released.

The Mechanics: What Has to Be Done

W E'LL GO THROUGH THESE ELEMENTS IN DETAIL in order in a moment, but here's an overview of what needs to get done in order. The questions most considered at this stage are:

Should your book be professionally designed?
What's all this business about ISBN number and barcodes?
Do I need a commercial distributor?

Well, there exceptions to every rule, but here are the "rules."

There is a sequence to how a book should evolve in the self-published world; here it is with a detailed explanation of the steps and the reason they're in this order will follow.

- Find and secure (sign an agreement) with a distributor
- Finish your book (but not necessarily edit it)
- Find an editor
- Find a book/cover designer
- Obtain 3 printing quotes
- Get an ISBN number
- Get Barcode number
- Get your book classified

Find/Secure a distributor—Right off the top, you do NOT need to have a finished book before securing a distributor. You should be looking for a distributor that has a catalogue of titles they represent and sales reps who are responsible to actually calling on customers—not just calling on the phone, but a sales staff that understands the value of face to face selling. The reason you want to find a distributor at this time is because the marketplace works far in advance of the finished book date.

Secondly, it's important to get a distributor at this stage because a lot of writers, according to Bill, wait until they have a book written, edited, cover designed and printed before they speak to a distributor. The absolute folly of this approach stems from one simple thing: what happens if Bill, the distributor/salesperson of your book, his salespeople and employees, and his customers—all of whom have a million years of book selling experience, what happens if any of them have any suggestions on how your book could be better? What happens if the color you've chosen for your book cover—say, green—is the one cover the industry knows makes people want to hurl? What happens is that you either fix whatever your distributor and his team feels strongly about (strongly means they feel whatever the problem is will impede their chances of successfully selling your book), or you can hope for the best and don't do anything.

That's one thing. You may wonder if you need a distributor and what criteria should you use to find one. If you're going to sell more than 1,500 copies (excluding friends and family), the answer is yes, you need a commercial distributor.

What does it cost to have a distributor? Between 28 and 32% of net receipts. Where do you find a distributor and what should you look for? In Canada, you can find a list of distributors by province by looking at the Canadian Association of Publisher's website: **www.publishers.ca**. In the US, you can to your local library and look through the Bowker's American Book Trade Directory. You can also go to **www.literarymarketplace.com**, a fantastic and helpful site.

The key thing behind a distributor is that this person will be your gateway to the world of book selling. This person will be your partner, so you had better have a good one. And don't forget, this is one of the times when you honestly don't know how to act: you may have a great book, in which case you're expecting royal treatment. On the other hand, it may indeed be you who should be kissing feet because they're the ones with the perspective: they've seen umpteen books throughout the years and their insights and suggestions predate, in most cases, the personal computer. The fact is, frankly, they've seen a million books before yours and you should just be happy ANYONE is talking to you about it and taking you seriously. Either way, stay cordial, polite and realize you need these people far more than they need you.

If you're writing a book on the monuments of Des Moines, Iowa, you don't need a distributor. Why? Because the vast majority, as in over 80% of your book sales, will be made within a 25-50 mile radius of Des Moines. In which case, you and your family and friends are now the distributor and are going to call on accounts and try to get the book taken on consignment, or approach a news seller/jobber in the area and see if they will do your distribution for you. The other 15 or 20% will find the book via your web site and search engines.

How does a distributor view books and their intended markets? Along these lines:

Regional books—There are regional books of regional interest and regional books of national interest. Skiing in Boulder, Colorado is of national interest. Church architecture in Boulder, Colorado is of both regional and national interest.

National books—History of the Vice presidents of the United States, for example, is of national interest, but it probably won't be a big international seller.

National/International books—The World's Best BBQ recipe can be of interest both nationally and internationally.

There are many questions you should ask before signing on with a distributor:

a. Do they have sales reps calling on the accounts that would be interested in your book? If they don't have sales reps, don't sign.

b. Do they produce a catalogue? Who do they mail it to?

c. Do they provide warehousing, shipping, collecting, either as a first or second party, and who do they do this through, how long have the second or third party been in business, and will they give you a list of clients to check references.

d. Do they have accounts with the major accounts—retail and wholesale?

e. Do they handle books in your subject field? The more books they have in your category, the better (they've established a rapport with the appropriate buyers)

f. The fee charged. Distributors can take between 28 and 32% of Net sales, Net is after applicable discounts.

g. Are there other charges? Warehousing, conventions, exhibits, restocking.

Be sure to get in writing the markets covered, i.e., libraries, university book store, mass merchants, wholesalers, religious book stores, new age, etc.

Finish Your Book—A lot of people think it's easy to write books if they like writing, and to prove it, they can show you the 3 books they've started and the half a dozen unfinished magazine articles. So, the challenge is to stick with it. I'd have to say writing your book is the easiest and certainly most enjoyable part of the exercise. A lot of people express amazement at the writing process, but if you have a sense of discipline and a sense of structure, meaning a path your book will follow, it's quite easy. There are a couple of pointers for those who haven't heard them before.

   a. **Create an outline**—Yes, this is English 101, but the more you've thought through your outline, the more the book will all but write itself. What do I mean by outline?

   i *Introduction:* what is your unique position/ stance/opinion and how will you be exploring/ explaining the subject. Think about how this subject will be addressed.

   ii What is the natural sequence of how you would explain the subject—is there a start, middle, conclusion? Then first things first, and this is your starting chapter.

   iii *Chapter 1:* What tools/materials do you need to rebuild the Briggs and Stratton engine you found at the bottom of your lake.

   iv *Chapter 2:* How to take the sucker apart without breaking key parts.

   v *Chapter 3:* How to organize the parts so you'll be able to get it all back together.

   vi *Chapter 4:* How to fix what ails it.

   vii *Chapter 5:* How to put the sucker back together.

   viii *Chapter 6:* Final check.

   ix *Chapter 7:* Give it a go!

b. **Research**—go to the book store, look on line, whatever you can do to ensure you're writing from a position of knowledge—otherwise you run the risk of writing for 8 months, spending some good money to publish your book, only to find out it is the 8th in a long line of books on the same topic.

c. **Competition**—what's the competition for your book, is there any, if so, what is it; what's worked, what hasn't; if not, how come?

d. **Discipline**—The best way I know how to get this done is to devote a specific time per day to write. Don't wait for inspiration to write or the publishing part of your book will be the least of your concerns, as you'll never finish it.

e. **Forget about spelling and grammar as you write**— just get the entire damn thing down before you start editing. Why? Because words and specific punctuation need context, something you won't be able to get the big picture on until the entire work has been ground through until the end. And if you stop and correct all spelling errors and grammar mistakes along the way, it is virtually a guarantee you'll never finish it. To quote Winston Churchill: *"You'll never make it to your destination if you stop and throw rocks at every dog that barks at you."*

Find an Editor—You either have to be very smart or very dumb to edit your own book. If you're somewhere in the middle, do the spell check, grammar check, have your friends read it over, have as many friends read it over as possible. Then, after all the changes have been suggested, ask your distributor for the names of some editors, or you could **Google** Freelance Editors Association and you'll be able to find a handful of editors near you.

There are two types of editors that you will be concerned about:

- Structural editors   - Copy editors

Structural editors will make sure the chapters (content) are organized for maximum reader comprehension.

Copy editors are looking for grammar, spelling, punctuation, suggesting placement of artwork, looking for consistencies of facts. They also deal with cover material and copyright data.

In theory, one would use a structural editor first and a copy editor second. For us self-published, always-mindful-of-what-it-costs authors, finding a copy editor who has experience with structural editing would cover everything. If you had to choose… choose the copy editor since they seem to encompass more, which means less work for you.

You could also look up www.literarymarketplace.com (**www.editors.ca** in Canada) on the web, an outstanding resource for writers. The nice thing about looking for an editor is you can choose one who you feel is appropriate to your subject matter, regardless of their location, as everything will be done by electronic file anyway. And don't forget: you have the final decision. It's easy to let "an expert" dictate how your book ultimately reads, which is something perhaps you should be leery about. No, I don't mean leery; I mean attentive to. It's your book; accept their input as suggestions, not as imperatives. It's not like they're the editor of Time Magazine and you're writing the cover story.

It's important to consider whether your book should have an index, in which case, you need an indexer. Your book designer will use one or suggest one. Some copy editors will also do this for you.

Find a Designer—I'm of the mind that we can't really be creative with the written word *and* the visual arts. You may be, of course. The best advice on whether or not to have a book/cover designer is whether you can afford it. There are book designers who will create a cover that will stand proudly next to the big boys on the store bookshelf, but they will cost. If you choose or are forced to do it yourself try not to let the book design get in the way of its potential success. Meaning, you'll be faced with enough hurtles along the way; don't need to be second-guessing something as important as book design.

Many first time authors question why they should spend money to have someone design their book cover and interior. It really boils down to where you plan on selling your book. If it's to the students of your karate class, who will buy the book anyway, it probably isn't necessary. If, on the other hand, you plan on taking a serious run at being an author and the book will be seen on TV interviews and in the best bookstores, then it's best to put the best foot you can afford forward.

The next section will deal with a handful of software programs that will, once you figure out how to use them, end up with the type of file most printers can use, but to help you decide whether to use a pro designer or not, think about whether you want to give your book a chance to stand up to the competition.

IMPORTANT: keep in mind the most important things about your book, all things considered:

- Cover front
- Outside back cover
  - Bullets (that's what these three points are)

- Quotes
- Tech info (establishes relevance to reader)
- Readable spine
- Copyright page for library sales
- Typeface style for the ages of your readers

Lastly, if you decide you'd like to use a professional designer and don't know any, you can test the validity of your distributor by asking them to suggest a couple: if they can't provide you with names of a couple of bonafide designers, consider another distributor.

The key consideration is for you to decide is your book going to be held back because of book design? Because, don't forget, the further your book gets from its original point of distribution and intent (your immediate customers) it will be judged solely on how it looks. Period. This is what's going to happen: you will be referred to a book designer or will find one in a directory. You will give him/her a disk with your entire book on it in a format they can use, with the pages and chapters broken up, grammar and spell check done. Say you've done a good job and have chosen a good designer who is upfront with you on how much time he/she will devote to your project. That's good because then they'll give you dates to have finished text with which to work.

Don't forget, the more changes you make—which is certainly your right, the longer it will take and the more it will cost. So don't lament how long your designer took if you kept on giving changes to her. I guess it makes sense, but the better you communicate what your book is about and some of the 'soft' facts', the faster and better this will go. By 'soft', I mean who's the book aimed at, what are some of your motives and hopes with the book, and so on. There's no question she will see pretty quickly the tone of the book, whether there's humor, whether it's strictly serious, and so on. Keep in mind that your designer is on your team—sometimes the 'little' facts are insights that give her the inspiration for your design. I say that partly from my own experience; I was very conscious of the fact I was dealing with a 'professional' and wanted to keep the time to a minimum, sometimes at the expense, I'm sure, of providing an in-depth glimpse.

Designing Software—There are two two main programs: Quark Xpress (around $1,000 US), Indesign (around $300), and some people still use Adobe Pagemaker ($500) US). I can't say much about these programs because, in truth, they make my brain bleed, because they're not the sort of programs you can just install and start using—you actually have to at least do the tutorial or take training. You may be more patient than I am, so good luck. I personally think you have far more important things to do that might help you sell your books than stay up late trying to figure out why the hanging indent on page 48 keeps falling off the page.

Find a Printer—There are book manufacturers and there are printers. Use a printer that prints books as their main business. If you have a distributor, before you print the book, your distributor will recommend various printers based on the type of book you're printing, from whom you should get three quotes. If your distributor doesn't know the name of three printers in your area, it's time for concern. Book printers have specialties: some specialize in cookbooks, 4-color, specialty binding, etc. Your distributor should know who the best printers are for your book at the best cost. Bill says he cannot tell how many times someone has come to him who have used the wrong printer and have paid three times more than they needed to have. Remember in book terms, getting your book printed is your biggest investment—it's the book version of buying a home.

There are certain things in the retail market place that are printing no-nos:

- Having your book spineless by wiro-bound (bookstores can't display it spine out)
- Children's book that are saddle stitched, i.e. are stapled instead of having a spine. Any book that is 32 pages or more can and should have a spine.
- There are certain types of books that need a lay-flat type of binding—craft books, cookbooks and manuals, etc. There are printers that can offer a binding that allows the book to lay flat, so any book that needs this type of binding that doesn't have it is a no-no.

Printers are obviously a specialized bunch, so usually your book designer will recommend one he/she has used in the past. Again, it's something you don't really want to worry about, meaning, choose a big, reputable company. Don't be tempted to use Harry's Discount Book Printing you found on the web that asked for a great deal of money upfront. It's just too scary knowing you're putting (probably) limited resources into this and a screw-up will be very harmful. And because it's your first time, you want people to be gentle with you, and you want to be able to believe in what people are telling you. I used Web COM for *Cook Like a Mother!* and Transcontinental for *Home Ec for the Domestically Challenged*. Anyway, they each treated me well, never spoke down to me (something that can happens a great deal when people realize they're speaking to a first timer), they followed the schedule they had set, the book was ready when they said it would be and obviously the quality was top notch. The biggest thing to watch out for: let's say your friend is a printing rep and he's promised you his company can—between printing jobs—print your book for cheap. The problem is you're behind the eight ball off the bat. I don't want for my first baby's schedule to be determined by whether they have a break in their schedule, and my first baby's treatment may be influenced by the fact it's a low cost thing. There's too much at stake for that. Make sure they'll be able to follow the schedule.

How to Choose a Printer—It may have become evident by now that writing, editing and publishing a book is harder and more complicated than you imagined. It's also probably become evident by now that if you had known how complicated and frustrating this process was going to be, you may have punted the entire concept and kept both your ideas and your money to yourself. Can't argue with you there.

But, assuming you're one of those people who won't take no for an answer—a trait that will pay big dividends during this entire process, I can assure you—and you're going to finish this one way or another. It's time to choose a printer.

So, is it best to go to your neighborhood Kinko's or Staples and ask them if they could print your baby? There's no shortage of print shops around the country, and they all do good work—in their field of expertise. Don't get sucked into using the same printer who does your favorite Chinese restaurant's flyers because you like the food. You're asking for more frustration than a) is necessary and b) you can take. Why? It's one thing waiting for things to happen when you know for a fact the company or individual knows what they're doing. It's another entirely waiting for something you're not sure will come out the way you expect it to.

If you're thinking of printing under 500 copies of your book and it's never really going to go face to face with a book that's been printed by book printing company, then consider using a company you can find on the internet if you Google "Print on demand". This is a printing process that takes a high resolution PDF file and photocopies and binds it. There are a few things to keep in mind. One, don't ever accept Print on Demand as a bona fide alternative to book printing. The cover, while accurate, still has only the quality of a copy—it would never compete face to face with a real printed cover. Two, the interior is also a copy, with the irregularities you find sometimes in a copy. But, if you are unsure how many books you need and you have the quality tolerance for it, then POD is great. It's a lot more expensive than conventional book printing—I recently printed about 30 POD books to get a jump on media coverage (real printing takes about a month), and each copy cost me about $8.00. Contrast that with the $1.06 I'm paying for my real printed book.

Some people swear by POD as a printing alternative. If you Google POD, as I mentioned, you'll get hundreds of thousands of sites. They talk about how great it is for you to be able to avoid spending a great deal of money upfront to print a quantity of books you can't be sure you'll sell, a very valid point. They also talk about printing only what you get orders for, also a very valid point. For me, the key factor is that a POD looks like a POD book—which, again, is ok, IF you don't plan to compete head to head with a conventionally printed book. Why? Hold the two of them up, side by side. One will look professional and the other one will look like a school project. In essence, the two points that, for sure, make sense, are, in reality, for people who aren't entirely committed to the self-publishing process. And by that I mean, if you and your distributor have decided that x number of books are a good quantity to print, you have committed to printing—and promoting and selling—those books. The POD option offers you an out, something you may want, enjoy or need; it says, "Hey, if it doesn't work, don't worry, you're not out a load of money on printing and at least you don't have a basement full off books." This is a very serious consideration, because there's no shortage of self-published authors who didn't keep at it, who have a stockpile of books.

So, getting back to my original point,

USE A PRINTER THAT SPECIALIZES IN BOOKS

Get an ISBN Number—what exactly is an ISBN number and why is it so important? By definition, it is the International Standard of Book Numbering. Think of it as the social insurance number for books, something that begins when it's created and dies when the book ceases to exist, and something that is the beginning and end of all classifications regarding your book. And as bizarre as it sounds, it's even more important than the title of your book or your name or the name of your publisher, if you have one. Without a social insurance number, you don't exist in the eyes of the government; same thing for the ISBN, without one, you don't exist in the eyes of the book industry.

That said, do you need one? If you want your book to be recognized by the book industry, as in, appear in major bookstores and libraries, the answer is yes. If you're printing 200 copies of Fido's Last Moments for your immediate family, the answer is no.

How do you get one? Very complicated, tough and secretive stuff here, as you'd expect for something as fundamental as an ISBN number. They're kept in a vault hidden away from prying eyes, accessed only by very high-ranking literary people. Just kidding, they're almost easier to get than a loyalty card.

In the US: The RR Bower Company, **www.bowker.com.**

In Canada: The National Library of Canada **www.**

nlc-bnc.ca. Both have reasonably quick turnaround, but count on 10-20 days to be safe. In other words, don't wait until the printer calls and says you need an ISBN number to get one.

Get a Barcode—Luckily, Barcodes, the things you'll find on almost every single item you buy—including your book—everywhere in the civilized world (and I use the word very liberally), are ordered and incorporated by your printer—you don't have to do anything. But to be safe, make sure it's on your checklist and that you confirm the printer has requested one. They may do it, but it's your ultimate responsibility to make sure it's there. The ISBN numbering system has been modified as of January 1, 2007, and is now a 13 number instead of the 10 digit they were previously. The intent of the change is to align the ISBN system with other product numbering, making trade with non-book retailers much easier.

On another note, when designing the cover, if you're using both bar codes, the barcode should appear on outside back cover.

Classifying Your Book—It is an undeniable truth that your book can only be in one section in the bookstore. Where should it be? Choose a main category, as in Business, New Age, Self-Help, Cooking, etc. The first category is the strongest, so let's say you wrote a book on how to improve your closing rate as a salesperson. Your first category is Business, second is Selling. Your two categories should be on the outside back cover.

Who Does What?

YOU KNOW WHAT AN AUTHOR DOES, as well as a designer, distributor, bookseller, and printer. But what is the difference between a publisher, distributor, wholesaler, jobber, and a retailer?

A **publisher** is someone who can decide to take on your book. They pay for the printing, cover design, editorial, etc. You receive an advance on royalties, plus a royalty rate based on the retail price. Normally this will be 8-10% for paper books. So, if your book retails $19.95, your royalty would be between $1.60 and $2. Your cash outlay is nil. Keep in mind it is very difficult to get your book placed with a publisher without having a literary agent to represent you.

Literary agents charge between 10-15% of the author's revenue. Almost all major publishing houses will not accept unsolicited manuscripts.

A **distributor** does the same thing as a publisher, in terms of sales marketing, warehouse and distribution, collection, conventions and exhibits, but does not pay to have the book printed, designed or edited. A distributor should have sales reps on the road, produce a catalogue, and be calling on customers physically (not exclusively by phone or mail).

A **wholesaler**, i.e., Ingram, Baker and Taylor (for the most part), are 'reactive' companies. If someone sends them an order, they'll fulfill the order. They will not actively seek orders, as they don't have a sales force. There are wholesalers who specialize in the retail book trade and those that specialize in the library marketplace; some specialize in both.

A **jobber**, in most cases, is a regional wholesaler that serves mass-market clients. Jobbers usually sell magazines with some books.

A **retailer** is the person who stocks and sells your book, the one who rings up the order and takes money from someone buying your book.

How to Set the Retail Price of Your Book

ALTHOUGH THIS IS SOMETHING YOUR DISTRIBUTOR will help you with, it's something you should know. Book pricing is a process of multiples—the retail price is a multiple over what you paid to have your book published. And don't forget, published means designed and printed. Something you may have gathered by now from Bill's sections, is the number of times a self-published author will take the notion of 'self' a little too literally. Meaning, the author will make every single decision by him or her self without the benefit of someone with experience. If you ever meet Bill at a book fair and you are fortunate to have a moment to chat with him (preferably over a drink or two—which you should buy, by the way, because you will benefit from a chat with him far more than he will ever benefit from a chat with you), he can regale you with a never-ending stream of mistakes made by well-intentioned, intelligent self-published authors. The most common mistake, from what I can gather, is pricing. So, here's what you should know about retail book pricing.

1. **Intelligence.** Gather whatever intelligence you can about other books that are similar. How are they priced? What do they offer? (Now, I know you've already done this research, so I'm not asking anything new.) How is your book different? What is the other books' page count? What is the trim size? How important is the sizing? If the other book is 6"x 10" and you can do yours at 5"x 8", it will be cheaper for you; but is their book a certain size for a reason? Find out. If the competition is

5″ x 8″, you can charge more for a 6″ x 9″, but the printing costs are more.

2. As mentioned, **publishers** (that's you, by the way) **work in multiples**. So, if the printer says it's going to cost you $3.00 a book, you should be looking at a retail price 6 to 8 times that number, or $18. or $24. suggested retail. Yes, you can do the Marketing 101 thing by turning $18. into $17.95. (I have to tell you, I wish I had this information before I priced Cook Like a Mother. The printing costs were around $3.00 a book. I priced it at $15. Bill's reps told me I had under-priced it (which, according to this formula, I did), but when you're the writer, publisher, editor, salesperson, PR and Promotion person, it becomes very evident very quickly that's it's tough to do everything.)

3. **Plan**—or be aware of—**returns**. The book industry is a manufacturers' nightmare: just because you sell it to the stores, does not mean they will sell it. That's why distributors have a 120-day payment schedule between the time they make the sale to the book industry and the time you receive a check. There are few things in life as demoralizing as seeing great news—your distributor has sold your book into all the major book stores and they owe you $10,000., only to see 3 months later that your publicity efforts didn't pan out and the returns equal $9,950. This is the book industry's version of "it ain't over until it's over." On a personal note, your distributor's efforts should become a call to arms for you, meaning, if your distributor's sales people have stepped up and found a way to sell your book, it REALLY behooves you to step up and find a way to publicize it. For timing questions, as in, when to do your publicity, see the section on Book Timelines.

Let's assume you've decided on a retail cost of $20. (Don't forget to make it $19.95/9). Here are the things you should know:

    a. Most distributors work on a 28-32% commission.
    b. The average large store discount is 48%

So, let's use the example to figure where the money's going:

Book retail cost:	$ 20.00
Store discount:	$ 9.60
Distributor and freight:	$ 3.16
Printing cost:	$ 3.00
Design and editing (one time cost)	$ 1.00
Advertising	$ 1.00
Total per book deductions:	$ 17.76
Total revenue per book:	$ 2.24
Second printing: (no design cost)	$ 3.24

The Web: Good Place to Buy Book Services?

If you had to look for an analogy for the difference between true self-publishing (you write the book, you find a distributor, you find an editor, you find the book and cover designer, you find the printer, you make arrangements to have the book delivered to your distributor, you make decisions on when and what happens, you do the publicity), and the myriad of Publishing companies you'll find on the web that are seductive with their "we-do-everything-for-you" offers, that would have to be home building. A lot of people interested in home building (not to be confused with home buying), do the research. There are certain things that must be done, as in, a house generally has 4 walls, a roof, indoor plumbing, electricity, and so on. There are different types of roofs, walls, construction styles, etc. So, a keener who feels they have the time and the confidence, might decide to become their own general contractor. They would do so because they would have ultimate control, the final say on everything. They would also do so to avoid the mark-ups that are inherent along the way.

But what about someone who's not that keen on learning or doesn't have the time or inclination? They'd find a builder. And this builder would make profits on everything, from nails to shingles to toilet seats. It may turn out, of course, that having a builder is the only choice you have, because you honestly don't have the time to devote to sourcing materials and workers. In this case, you'd have to live with the fact that you are using an interpreter for your work. You are using a middleman.

This is the way I view companies that offer to publish your book on the web. To name a few:

1ˢᵗ Books.com (now authorhouse.com)
iUniverse.com
PublishAmerica.com
Trafford.com
Infinity Publishing.com

The terms to keep in mind are "vanity publishing" and "subsidy publishing." A lot of people use these terms interchangeably with "self-publishing," but this isn't accurate. Why? Because the first two terms refer to you, the writer, giving a company money to publish your book. With self-publishing, you have 2 key differences: 1, you're able to 'shop' for prices, and 2, the pricing doesn't include profit and overhead. Vanity publishing is considered expensive for this reason, and because you are "forced" to accept how they wish to price their services. I.e., you may choose a company that says they will create, edit, print and sell your book for $10,000. This fee includes 10 hours of editing, 4 hours of cover design, 2 hours of book design, and so on. Super. But what happens if you need 15 hours of editing, 6 hours of cover design, and so on? The overage rate is generally highly punitive, so you'll end up paying far in excess of the $10,000 you liked in the first place.

Lastly, it's a matter of control. You'll never know if the designer working on your book has done similar books to yours, or if the editor has ever edited a book like yours. Meaning, they wouldn't be your top choice if you were doing the choosing. The nice thing (read: effective) about self-publishing, is your distributor will more than likely be the one referring you to editors, designers, printers—that are relevant to what you're doing. If you're doing a cookbook, he/she will recommend printers who have done cookbooks and offer the binding most appropriate for cookbooks.

But to put this into context, recently a friend of a friend called and said she was trying to decide whether she should use one of the web sites that are listed first if you Google "self-publishing." If you've done the search, you know about 318,000 sites come up. So, let's call her "Roberta." We discussed for quite a while the merits of true self-publishing versus a company saying all you have to do is write the book and send it and money to them.

There are an almost limitless number of companies with web sites devoted to helping you with all facets of book publishing. Once you know enough about self-publishing to know there are many steps and you realize you are, in effect, the general contractor, you may begin to look at turnkey alternatives. Let me describe briefly "Roberta's" situation because it will help you gain a perspective on why one would consider the turnkey option versus the general contractor option.

Roberta runs a clinic that has something to do with understanding anger in one's life (I'm not a very good listener if I'm in the middle of writing something). Her clinic is very busy and there's going to be a nationally televised program that deals with what her clinic offers soon. She has a web site that her advertising directs people to qualify them for her clinic. What do these three elements indicate? Two things: one, she has a built-in distribution/sales centre, with the ability to sell to people who come to her clinic and visitors to her web site. Two, she's going to have national interest in what she's doing, directing further people to the two distribution/sales centers. All this means she's busy. She wants the least onerous route of self-publishing, even if it means forfeiting strategic advantages of being a general contractor.

In my very feeble mind, I'd have thought a better alternative for Roberta would have been to have her book professionally designed, print a couple of hundred POD (see the section on Printing), get a distributor who would list the book on all directories and Bob's your uncle: she keeps control of her book AND the ultimate/potential distribution of it. The key detriment of using a one-stop shop is that they will assign one of their own ISBN numbers, a seemingly innocuous thing that unfortunately all but precludes your ability to find and secure a distributor.

The Web: Good Place to Sell Your Books?

THERE'S NO QUESTION YOU SHOULD INDEED have a website, for a number of reasons:

1. It's a terrific reference point for people who want to consider your book—the media, bookstores, potential speaking engagers, etc.
2. It's not entirely a terrific sales tool, for a couple of reasons:
   a. Even though the payment system you'll probably use will be Pay Pal, a very secure payment processing service, people are still a little shy about giving credit card info and the such on big name sites, let alone smaller, weenie ones.
   b. My personal experience has been for every 1,000 hits, I get 1 book sale, which is probably the worst sales conversion ratio on the planet. Why is the conversion so low? Hard to say. It may be in the design of the site, which might be lacking a compelling reason to buy.
3. Is a must for credibility. It's gotten to the point with web sites that the perception is: if you don't have one, are you really the expert you say you are?

Should you have your site professionally designed?

I think so. Learning code and html uplinks, etc., is a lot to learn, so say nothing of learning how the average person views websites and what influences them to carry on to purchase something.

The Real Work: Marketing/Advertising/ Publicity/Promotion

I F YOU'RE AT THIS POINT IN THIS BOOK, it's either because you're honestly at this stage of development—you've written, designed or had designed your book, and it's being or has been printed—or you're just nosy to see what comes next. I hope it's the former, because you deserve a pat on the back. This business is so gut wrenching, ego flattening, demoralizing and stacked against the little guy, to say nothing of expensive, you have to take accomplishments wherever you can—and celebrate them. Inexpensively, of course. If you were to buy your favorite wine every time your book got placed in a new store or you got a review or radio/TV interview, I think it would cost more than the designing and printing combined. So, you have to be judicious with your self-supportiveness, something that's as hard to do, as it is to contemplate.

They say you're supposed to do promotion and publicity even before your book is written. I'm not sure I buy that. Reviewers are so whacked out of their brains trying to cover actual books sitting chin-high on their desks, I sincerely doubt whether they'll spend the time to look through a partial manuscript. Don't forget, I'm still speaking of the self-published world here. Things would be different if your name was TL Kowling and you used really faint ink on the cover so the reviewer might confuse you with JK Rowling, but let's not get too silly.

Perhaps the most important thing for you to keep in mind is that this is a game. This entire thing is a game and it behooves you to figure out how to play. The following is a step-by-step guide to how to do the real work, but it's also determined, as I guess all things are, by your attitude. To find the perfect balance between knowing the media is like a huge open throat, constantly hungry to be fed, and playing the game their way so you can be considered fodder, is, quite frankly, the most challenging and rewarding game to play.

Marketing Plan

The ostensible importance of a marketing plan is that it enables you to have a track to run on. It will force to you take a long, hard look at how much resources you have to devote to the marketing and advertising part (publicity is by nature non-paid). In reality, though, the importance of a Marketing plan is that it demonstrates to your distributor's sales reps you're serious about your book. It's important to repeat (because I've probably said this a thousand time to anyone who will listen), it's not so much what other people do that will determine the success of your book; it's what YOU do. So, if you write a marketing plan and give it to your distributor who can give it to his/her reps who can show it to book buyers, YOU have a leg up over some schlep who merely wrote a book and is constantly asking her distributor "so, did you sell any of my books today!!!?"

What does a marketing plan look like?

This is where you give serious, objective thought to your book and its place in the market.

Intended Market—Who is the intended reader? What do they like to read, do, etc? Be fairly specific. The more you know who you think will read your book, the better.

Budget—How much do you have to spend on this?

Media—What media have you chosen, why, what spending levels? For each media.

Timeline Grid—People (buyers) love to see grids; they look more official and professional. If you prepare a media plan with grid, people think you're serious and know what the hell you're doing.

Example—I've included an example of a media plan on pages 54 and 55, as well as a sample Press Release on page 53.

Advertising

Approach

Right off the bat, don't commit the same blunder so many other authors make: writing crappy marketing copy to describe your book. After spending as long as you probably have to write the book, the press release, the back cover, and on and on, there's a tendency to skimp on marketing copy. Big mistake. It may be you don't have the writing style or skill to get it done, so hire someone. Where do you need strong writing?

- Ads
- Information sheets
- Catalogue
- Press release

There's no question that the more money you have to devote to advertising, the better. The rule of thumb is to include $1.00 to the cost of each book (your cost) for advertising. Here are some additional considerations:

- Add to the book reviews you're getting with promotional activities and advertising in the book sections of major newspapers.
- It's also smart to consider the different target audiences. Think about the people you really think will read your book and then give thought to who does

the buying for these people (don't be naïve enough to think the primary user is always the primary buyer.

- Choose the classified sections to advertise in. They're much cheaper than the rest of the paper.
- Buy advertising in specialized newspapers. This goes back to knowing who the primary buyer is of your book. Specialized newspapers can be less expensive (from a cost per thousand (CPM) perspective which is the standard measure of how advertising is bought) than major national newspapers. It's not always the case, though; sometimes the niche market they fulfill is so unique you have to pay a premium to get in.
- Get the attention of the reader with a strong headline; without one, you've reduced the potential reader of your ad by half (newspaper readership surveys indicated that 50% of readers skim the paper until they find a headline that grabs their attention.
- Design your ad to look like an editorial.

Testimonials have a greater draw than straight copy. Bear in mind you should have at least 5 points you want to get across over and over again:

- Why is your book unique?
- What are you saying that others have not, how is it different otherwise?
- Have experts in the field read your manuscript and have given quotes to use either throughout the book or on the back cover?
- Do you see your book as leading a trend or expanding on information that's already been covered?

Media Grid
Using a media grid similar to what the big ad agencies use is

a help if you're an organized person and like to have a grip on these types of things. Below is a press release. On the next page you'll see one with the calculations explained.

For Immediate Release

Contact: Kate Bandos at KSB Promotions: 800-304-3269 or
kate@ksbpromotions.com

Cooking and cleaning advice for the "domestically-challenged"

Give a man a fish and he eats today. Teach a man to fish and he can feed himself for the rest of his life.

It's arguable that no one feels this saying more keenly than someone who suddenly has to cook for his family – whether it's a newly divorced dad or a husband whose wife is away for the weekend. Making dinner for yourself can be as simple as you want; making dinner for children who need proper nutrition is another matter. The easy decisions a competent cook makes every day can cause great anxiety in someone who is suddenly responsible for all the meals.

Peter Wright, a single father with joint custody of his two boys for more than 7 years, had to face many such decisions. He wishes he had paid more attention to how his mother made tasty, nutritious meals – magically, it seemed – every single day. Peter became determined to learn to cook the meals he grew up with. There were many panic calls to Mom with questions like:

Taylor, Peter and Spencer

- How do you prepare a chicken for roasting?
- How can you tell when things are cooked?
- How can you tell when things are bad and shouldn't be eaten?
- How long can leftovers stay in the fridge?

It's very stressful trying to be good at something you haven't been taught. These experiences led him to write **Cook Like a Mother! Clean Like a Pro! The Single Dad's Guide to Cooking and Cleaning**. Now, anyone who's suddenly in charge of Domestic Duties can get a running start without the steep learning curve. Peter offers down-to-earth advice on:

- How to stock a kitchen for maximum flexibility
- What kitchen gadgets to get – and avoid
- Cooking tips to help anyone "cook like a mother"
- Professional food handling tips, cooking temperatures
- Desserts that are easy to make and kid favorites
- Products and approaches that speed up the clean up

> *The Cook Like a Mother Directive: avoid asking girlfriends or wives—existing, ex, or upcoming, any questions about how to prepare the meal we're cooking. This is our chance to prove we're capable.*

Recipes in **Cook Like a Mother!** are written for people doing something for the first time: **What You'll Need** details all the ingredients and **What You'll Do** details what, and in what order, you have to do – for taste and health. There are many "gems" or tips that can turn an ordinary meal into a Mom-like meal, and they're all expressed in an easy-to-follow, light-hearted fashion. "As a card-carrying cooking non-keener, the book is written the way I'd want things explained to me," explains Wright, "with sports and tool analogies throughout. I think the trick to getting good at something is to not take yourself too seriously in the beginning."   over . . .

1-866-261-4441   www.cooklikeamother.com

Markets	Dates		Magazine			Flyers
			Cost/Ad	# of Ads	Total Cost	Cost/1,000
Detroit			100.00	4	400.00	0.03
Toronto			100.00	4	400.00	0.03
Dayton			50.00	4	200.00	0.01
Thunder Bay			50.00	4	200.00	0.01
			This column ⟶	times this column ⟶	equals this column ⟶	same ⟶

The purpose of this grid, of course, is to allow you to create an advertising plan and know exactly which markets and media you can afford. To create this type of grid, use a speadsheet program and do the following calculations in the grid above.

Note: The rates here are totally fictious be sure to take your heart medication before getting real rates.

# of Flyers	Total Cost (in 1,000s)	Newspaper Cost/Ad	# of Ads	Total	Radio Cost/Ad Cost	# of Ads
20,000	600.00	100.00	4	400.00	20.00	5
20,000	600.00	100.00	4	400.00	20.00	5
20,000	200.00	50.00	4	200.00	5.00	5
20,000	200.00	50.00	4	200.00	5.00	5
thing →	here →	same →	thing →	here →	same →	thing

Publicity

Let's get one thing straight: this is a game, a very complex game you will be striving to perfect for a long time. It's also a lot of work, and I mean a lot. Because this is the Insider's Guide, I'm going to share with you some publicity gems that worked for me, along with some tidbits I've gleaned over the past couple of years from other authors who have done a good job in getting the name of their book out there.

The first thing you need to do is write a press release.

How do you write one? What do you focus on? Let's consider who the intended reader is. Any media you can think of, from the Boobtown Banner to NBC, receives hundreds of faxed and mailed press releases a day, so it's not only a matter of actually writing the releases and sending them, it's a matter of thinking how you can position your book—or something about your book—that will make the editor feel their readers/viewers need to know about it. But before you start to write your press release, write a:

Fact sheet

A fact sheet states the basic facts about the book—title, author, publisher, size, ISBN number, number of pages, publication date and binding. Of course, it would be beneficial to include some tidbits from the book that might entice the editor to open the book.

How to write a press release:

1. Make sure the release has a grabby headline. It needs to grab the attention of the editors as well as the readers. Ideally, your press release should reflect topics of interest to the readers or viewers the editors are concerned about, topics that can be addressed by your book.

2. Use a news style favored by reporters and editors: tell it in an inverted pyramid format. Meaning, the piece should start with THE most important element, then the second, then the third and so on.

3. It's important to speak the language of the intended audience. If your book has more than one key audience, it might be a good idea to write up a press release to address each audience.

4. A great tactic is to approach a media with a local element, if you can find/create one. What is meant by a local element? Well, let's say you've written a book for beginner cooks—hey, like mine!—and you feel your book would be appropriate for college students. If the market you're approaching is a college town, you could approach the local media with a press release that starts with something about the fact that the majority of their college students gain weight the first year because of poor nutrition decisions.

5. **Pitch letter.** The pitch letter is a perfect example of the need to make editors' lives easy by triggering a story in their mind. Don't make them have to use their creativity to find an angle on how your book applies to their readership. Ideally, the pitch letter would be tailored for each media, because otherwise, how could you make sure you're going to plant a story in the editor's mind of relevance to their readership.

6. It's important to remember to include a review copy of the book, not waste your time with excerpt pages. Never forget that editors get a thousand books a year and if your excerpts have to compete with someone else's complete book, I believe you'll lose every time.

7. Another effective technique is to create return labels that say something clever/targeted about your book.

8. There are three types of columnists you should work with:

a. **Local**—Working with local columnists can be a great way of ensuring coverage—if you make their lives easier by helping them with story ideas. These local columnists make a great effort to support local businesses or initiatives and love to receive interesting stories they can write about you.

b. **Specialized**—Most newspapers have columnists that cover gardening, parenting, travel, and so on. Does your book help these people in their quest to constantly be supplying their readers with themed stories? Get the book into these people's hands.

c. **Syndicated**—There are over 1,600 columnists who write syndicated columns about everything from car repair to sex to outdoor living to how to choose an RV. Is your book a great fit with a homogeneous audience that has their own magazine? That's who you want to get your book in front of. The best way of finding syndicated columnists is to Google them.

There are many types of press releases, and we will deal with 6 examples.

a. **A print media press release**—This is a press release primarily for the book and magazine reviewer. This usually will be sent with a finished copy of your book, addressed to the book reviewers. Using the person's name ensures the book ends up on their desk. Addressing your package to "Book Reviewer" ensures the most junior person in the department will get it. Press release and book goes to reviewer a minimum of 5 weeks before publication date. This press release features the unique content of your book: why it's different from other books on the same subject matter, a couple of feature salient points the book contains. The second part of the press release features the authors' information, such as previously published books, magazine articles, media appearances, and other information that establishes the authors' credibility and credentials. If you have hired a freelance publicity and promotional person, the press release will finish off with contact info for interviews.

b. **Electronic media**—This press release goes out 3 weeks prior to the publication date. This features media credentials, which demonstrates the producers won't be concerned about how you are behind a mike or in front of a camera. The second part features the book, as per the above press release.

c. **Targeted market release**—As an example, if you're doing a sports book, your material should go to the sports editor. If you've written a cookbook, your book and material should go to the Food Editor. If you've written a lifestyle book, it should go to, I'll bet you've guessed by now, the Lifestyle editor. This is sometimes a bit of a challenge for books that have two categories. My first book was a perfect example of that. Cook Like a Mother made the newspapers think it should go to the Food Editor. Clean Like a Pro/The Single Dad's Guide to Cooking and Cleaning made them want to send it to the Lifestyles editor. My recommendation on this is YOU have to be decisive and know exactly where you'd like your book to be reviewed. Yes, you want it reviewed period, but no, you don't want the wrong section reviewing it. Case in point, one newspaper, a very influential one, reviewed my book in the Food section. Well, I'm the first to admit I'm not blazing new ground with my recipes, hell, I'm happy to be able to make meals my kids want to eat. But the point is this reviewer sort of shat on my cooking parts, and although he extolled the kids' parts and cleaning stuff, it was very clear it should have been reviewed in the Lifestyles section—as all the other papers in the US and Canada had done.

d. **Special markets releases**—Let's say you've done a book called "Getting the Most out of your Employees", and you think your book has potential to be used by a corporation or an industry, you might send 25-30 copies off to the President of the company or VP of Human Resources along with a letter, because most large companies will pay for speakers to come in and address such issues, or they'll buy copies to send to their regional offices. This press release will refer to a couple of selected points ("How to Retain Present Employees and make them Happy, see page 47"). You can choose the best single line selling points and highlight them; doing so will increase the chances of your book actually being opened and read.

e. **Other print media press release**—You have two objectives here. One, you're looking for a review. And two, if your release mentions "excerpt rates are available". This way they may pay for excerpts or commission you to write an article based on your expertise.

f. **Seasonal press release**—This press release is if your book is good for, say, Mother's Day or Thanksgiving. Here is when you could do a small mailing targeted to Lifestyle editors who are always looking for material to fill these holiday themes. The press release has to immediately establish to the editor why your book fits into the subject matter.

Let's say you've written a kids book. Let's give this some thought. Where can you get coverage?

Newspaper—Parenting section. Lifestyle section

Magazine—You now have to make a list of all the newspapers that have a Parenting section or when they have a feature on Parenting. They may just have a Lifestyle section.

So, I'm going to outline the things I've done that have allowed me to achieve over $150,000 of media exposure, in this order:

1. Write a 3ʳᵈ party Press Release
   a. Something that follows this guideline: it's written as though written by someone else, and attempts to find a balance between obviously selling your book and highlighting the issues inherent in your subject matter. That may sound like doubletalk, but the challenge you face lies in appealing to the media that the topic or area of interest you've covered is indeed either newsworthy, topical and/or interesting.
   b. In all honesty, they couldn't give a rat's ass about why you wrote your book—unless it's an interesting story. They couldn't care about your background—unless it's an interesting story. They only care about one thing: will it pique their readers/viewers/listeners' interest, or, will it make for interesting copy, TV or radio.
   c. The book is secondary. It's kind of like Zen: the closer you get to why you're doing something, the harder you try, the more you will be shunned and the further away you will be from getting the media coverage you need.

2. Write a **Praise For page**
   a. This Praise For page thing came a little late to me, I'm disappointed and bummed to report. I used to send out a book with as many accumulated reviews as I had. The problem with this approach is twofold: 1),

you don't want to person to have to thumb through entire pages of newspaper looking for the sections you've highlighted.

b. This is I'll admit a little tricky if you don't have any reviews yet, but you're going to have to be creative. Think of and approach the people who offer creditability and are sympathetic to your cause (I was going to say supportive but sympathetic is probably more easily achieved). Tell them exactly what you're doing and why you'd like their input. Ask if you can quote them. And just because you don't have friends who are reviewers for the New Yorker, you may have a friend who's President of the local chapter of a charity that's relevant to your story/message. For example, let's say you've written a book about a family of cancer survivors who are a source of inspiration to everyone who hears about them. Your story is touching, sensitive and provides a comprehensive view of ontological treatment. You could speak to the Head of Oncology for that hospital or treatment center.

c. Think of people who are informed and credible. Bear in mind this is a perspective issue: if you think you honestly will be providing a service for anyone who's just been diagnosed with the illness (I know, I may have chosen quite possibly the worst example), then you can feel confident in approaching relevant people for their feedback to your book. In all circumstances you're going to have to be respectful of their time, but don't come off like you're imposing on them just for the sake of commence. This goes back to the next point about being a salesperson—while you will indeed benefit from their positive words, you cannot forget the fact that so many readers will benefit from your words.

3. You're a Salesperson now.

   a. Regardless of what you were before, regardless of what your job was while you were writing your book, you are now a salesperson. Forget the fact that you're a published author. You're a sales person, and a good salesperson knows their market. They know, for example, if the book is on ancient glass-blowing techniques, the history of glass, when it became widespread, how it evolved, and so on and so on. They know minute details about why some cultures are afraid of glass (if they are, it's news to me), they would know where the best glass is made, where the crappiest glass is made. They would know all these things.

   b. Why? Because it would give them creative fodder for a Press Release: "History to be rewritten—Cleopatra's death has been kept a secret. She actually died walking through a pane of glass." A good salesperson would know how many amateur glass blowers there are in the world. They'd know why people get into it; they know why it's so difficult.

   c. Again why? Because YOU will have to believe so strongly that you offer the world (or at least your market) something they need and will be improved by reading so you'll be fuelled day in, day out to keep after that Lifestyles Editor. It has to become a battle for you, a battle you refuse to lose. Because, the fact is, if you give in, you indeed did lose—you lost valuable media exposure.

   d. And don't forget: never think they're not covering you because your book sucks; think they're not covering you because you haven't thought of a good enough approach. This entire venture is on your shoulders.

   e. So, most important: Don't give up, and equally important: Buy a database of media contacts.

4. **Prepare your sales kit**

   a. Buy some of those shiny presentation folders that have two sleeves.

   b. Buy a package of full page labels

   c. Get your book designer to provide you with an electronic version of your book cover so you can make your own labels.

   d. The trick is to set up a system that enables you to move as quickly as possible: your database should be able to mail merge, print labels and create follow-up phone lists without any difficulty.

   e. Keep mailing envelopes stocked.

   f. Find out what the postage is to mail your particular book and buy those stamps.

   g. Ultimately, you want to create a sales kit and approach that allows you to get a lead (when you think of a publication, say) and without any hoo-hah at all, get your book in the mail.

5. From Small to Big

   a. Most places have local media, especially newspapers. This is the best way to start. Why? Because independent of literary merit, they will cover your book because you're a local author.

   b. By the same token, most regions have media that's oriented towards them. Again, the same principle applies: you're a regionally local author. There are more and more radio and TV groups, to say nothing of newspaper, that cater to a region, groups that are made up of many smaller media outlets. Getting them to cover your book fro their region is a big plus.

   c. Once you're figured out who the local, then regional players are, you can figure out whom the national players are.

6. First things first

   a. Here's a little game you'll like playing. It's called "Who Do you Call First." It's a great game. Here's how you play it. Decide on what city area you want media coverage in. Then decide on a bookstore, usually the biggest. Approach them and introduce yourself as a new author wanting to hold an event in their store. While you have to be nice about it, you also have to realize they want to sell books too, so although they may demonstrate a little bit of an attitude because you're not JK Rowling, understand they want to sell books too. Now, the next part of the game is to approach every single media in that area/market and tell them you're having a book signing at their local store. Who do you speak to at the specific media? Radio: find the program/host that best reflects your potential reader. Newspaper: find the appropriate section editor. TV: find the line-up editor or news director. The bigger the market you're approaching, the more difficult it is to get through, so don't get discouraged. Again, it's time to be nicely persistent.

7. Be a Hoarder

   a. If you don't have a copy of anything you do in the media, it might as well have not happened. You've got to remember to get copies of everything so you'll be able to put together a killer sales kit.

8. Some **publicity gems**

   a. An interesting thing happened to me while seeking quotes for my back cover. I thought it would be really helpful if I had some media quotes, in addition to my expert quotes, so I sent the advance copy to a couple of high profile radio and TV talk show hosts. As a matter of fact, both of them have programs that are number one in their respective timeslots for their respective media. And an interesting thing happened: each of them replied that they wouldn't be giving me a quote, because they don't do that sort of thing, but each of them said they'd have me on their show. I know people who have tried for ages to get on their shows and to no avail, so this is an interesting, serendipitous, shall we say, way of doing things.

b. Media tour gem: The first time I did a dedicated media tour for Cook Like a Mother!, I did the obvious things: contact the book store, arrange a book signing event, approach the local media—newspaper, TV and radio—and either sit in my hotel room or go rollerblading when I wasn't preparing or sleeping. For Home Ec for the Domestically Challenged, I decided to make full use of the time I was going to be in each city. (I also bought a travel trailer RV so I wouldn't have to incur outrageous hotel and airfare bills, but that's a different story.) So, my goal was to find local events that were appropriate for my subject, or if they didn't exist, create them. How can you do that? Well, think of a local charity that would appreciate some awareness raising, and then think of how you could create a promotion that would benefit it. If you realize that local media, especially in smaller towns are looking for ideas that they could take to a local advertiser in search of incremental ad revenues, then it becomes simply a creative process to come up with a promotion. If you then realize that local chains or big stores are looking for ways that help them stand out in the community in a good way, then it's up to you to create something that makes sense and can be done relatively easily. The obvious great thing about this approach is if it flies, and there are no guarantees it will, it benefits you, the local media, the local advertiser, the local charity and the local residents that end up a little enriched by whatever it is you're doing.

More than likely, this will be the first time you'll be on radio or TV. It's very exciting, I have to say. Because trying to coach first-timers in interview skills could be—and has been—the topic of entire books, I'm just going to address some things I hope will serve you well.

Above all be completely in the moment. Meaning, know what you want to say, why you're there and stay focused—one moment thinking of something else during an interview and you will seem far dumber than you really are. Let's start with:

Radio interviews

As with all media, you have to be prepared—and have a clear idea of what you're trying to achieve. When I first started promoting *Cook Like a Mother!*, I thought the media coverage was the aim, the goal. Sure the book sold, but my real aim should have been to enable the host and me to sell the book, as in, how does the book help people, why is it relevant, what are the key messages, and so on. TV is pretty straightforward: you try to look confident, clear-headed, knowledgeable and gracious. Radio is a little different. You have the live aspect of TV, but the preparation aspect of print. Meaning, you can have notes, key messages, etc. The thing that's really worth remembering for any media, but especially live electronic, is that people want to be entertained; if you end up informing or educating them at the same time, it's a plus the hosts and producers will appreciate, but you HAVE to entertain. I also can't stress enough the idea of key messages. When you watch a politician, especially a very high level one, like President Bush, it's not readily apparent unless you're watching for it how well they've been trained to stick to their key messages. For instance, when the decision was made to go to war with Iraq and reporters would question his decision, his key message was that Hussein was a bad man, terrorism had to be stopped and freedom is worth fighting for. Regardless of what a reporter asked, the answer would come back in the form of these three—unarguable—truths.

It's also important to stress that doing media in areas whose bookstores haven't stocked your book is like taking the time to select, order and pay for the best steaks you can buy, telling everybody about them and making sure they'll all show up, at a time when there's no propane in the BBQ or no means to cook them: YES you got the best steaks, YES you spiced them to perfection, YES they would have been the best and YES you got great coverage, YES you did a great interview, YES you created demand for your book, but NO the book wasn't available and the people who gave their name in to have the book ordered will invariably forget why they were in that store and why they were interested in a book whose title they've forgotten anyway. Everyone's familiar with that expression "all publicity is good publicity", but the only caveat or qualifier I'd insist on is make sure your book's not only available in local stores, but physically accessible, meaning they're actually in the stores.

A great tip during a radio interview is to tell the host (and his/her listeners) that in a minute you'll give them the top three tips taken from your book.

TV

Without question, the big prestige and awareness comes from TV. From arranging the interviews to how to do them well, consider the following:

- Allow about 4-5 weeks lead-time. Meaning, you can begin approaching electronic media once your book is scheduled to be in the stores in a month.
- When you call and are speaking to the TV station receptionist and ask for the segment producer or line-up editor for the noon or morning news program. Don't rely on a list of contacts; make your own.

Ask to speak to the person; if you don't get through, leave a compelling message and say that you'll be sending your book and press kit for them—and make sure you send it out that day.

The Daily **DO IT** Rule

BY NOW YOU'VE PROVEN TO YOURSELF YOU CAN do most things right. You've had the discipline to write your book, you've found a designer who's made your book look great, you've chosen a printer who's done a good job, and your distributor's done their job and the book's in stores. You know how to create a press kit and what has to be done to coordinate book events with media coverage.

It could be argued that the next thing you have to do is the most difficult. If you're the disciplined type, this will be easy. All you have to do is devote 30 minutes per day on something to further your book. By something, what do I mean?

- Contemplate corporations who might benefit from having your book as a gift to clients/sales people, etc. Make a list and begin a systematic approach.
- Contemplate specialty media that may offer a great opportunity for exposure.
- Look through your Press Release and accompanying material and tweak.
- Look through your Press Release and tailor it to specific media that represents different potential readers of your book.
- Send out press materials—there will always be some media you haven't approached, or media you haven't approached in a while.
- Think of an article you could write and send to an appropriate media.

What I'm trying to convey is that you can't wait for inspiration or when you may feel like doing this crap. It has to be done every single day—well, maybe you can take the weekend off.

Why is it so important to follow the Daily Do-it Rule? Because it's too easy to give up. It's too easy to say I'll do it next week; I'll make up the time I missed. Lastly, why is this rule the utmost guarantor of success? Because I can't imagine not being successful if you do this. The proof of success is whether you sell all the copies of your book, and you owe it to yourself not to have a basement full of books.

The Whens: Industry Timing

THIS SECTION DEALS WITH WHEN YOU SHOULD be doing things, based on when you'd like to do things, as in, when you'd like your book to hit the bookstores shelves.

You might feel you can get your book out in 90 days, something that's physically possible if you don't want to sell it to anyone. The realistic timeline is minimum 10 months. Let's assume your book is coming out in October. In Jan and Feb, you should be looking for a distributor. A distributor doesn't need a finished book to sell. The reason you want to find a distributor at this time is because the marketplace works far in advance of the finished book date. For example, from the time the sales people present your book to Ingram's, Barnes and Noble, Indigo, there's lapse of between 90 to 120 days. Keep in mind also that your distributed has to load your title into the major databases in North America a minimum of 30 days before the salesperson goes in to solicit the order. The accounts that require this are Ingram, Barnes and Nobel, Borders, Baker and Taylor, Costco, Books a Million, Sam's Club, etc.

So, you have found a distributor by the end of February. Next step, between January and March, you should have a designer. Designers can be hired for only the front cover, the back cover, both, or just the interior (see Designer section). Finished cover design must be done by March 30th. Beginning of April, you should be interviewing freelance publicity people before they get booked up as the season nears (see Publicity section). By the May 1st, you have printers' quotes, preferably 3 (see Printers section). By May 15, you should have your preliminary design and editing done. By May 30th, you should select your printer and sign contract. By June 1st, you should have between 20 and 30 copies of your book printed by a

Print on Demand printing company that can print from a High Resolution PDF file. Why? You will send these advance copies out to people who can give you quotes/endorsements to be included on your outside back cover. There are certain newspapers that will only review from proofs (formerly referred to as galleys)*: NY Times, Chicago tribune, LA, and Publishers Weekly. You may also want to send these advance proofs to magazines for serialization or excerpts. On July 20th, book goes to printer. On July 25th, press release for print media should be completed and finished books arrive at distributor's warehouse by August 15th. Between August 15th and 25th, review copies are sent to print media with press releases. Aug 23rd, to the end of the 1st week of September, press release and books are sent to the electronic media.

Books start appearing in the bookstores the last 10 days of September.

Your official publication date will always be a Saturday, unless it's a cookbook, which will have a Thursday publication date. Most people get confused about *finished* book date and *publication* date. *Finished* book date allows the media the time to review your book in time for the *publication* date. North America media is well known for honoring the publication date. From the time the books are sent to the stores and reviewers have had a chance to review it, it takes between 4 to 6 weeks. All your interviews, appearances, etc., start on your ***publication*** date, NOT BEFORE.

Nothing annoys a distributor more than a client who calls and asks "if I delivered my books to you last week, how come they're not in the stores yet?" There is a discipline and a time schedule to book distribution: calling on bookstores, waiting

---

* in essence, these are mock-ups of your final book—they've been edited, book-designed and so on, they just aren't in their final bookstore version

for the order, receiving your books, sending your books to the stores that bought them, and the stores actually getting them onto the shelves, all takes time, time that cannot be compressed—even though, as new self-published authors, we want things to happen NOW.

Remember, as Bill Hushion has told me a fair number of times, you can only be a literary virgin once; meaning, you can only have one publication date that everyone (distributor, media, book stores, etc.) is aware of, respecting and working towards. If, for some reason, you know you're not going to be able to keep the original schedule, it is IMPERATIVE you notify your distributor for a couple of reasons:

1. a new publication date can be rescheduled
2. the distributor can go to the major accounts and seek extensions on your purchase orders so they're not cancelled. You would be amazed how many self-published authors will not notify their distributor that the initial deadline cannot be kept, and as a result, the books arrive in the distributor's warehouse 90 days after they were supposed to, the author has been asked to do interviews, which they do, without any books in the stores. When the distributor goes to ship the books out, they will be sending out 50% of what the initial expectation was because of inevitable cancellations. Your lack of communication can single-handedly ensure your book will fail.

Please note most retail purchase orders have a cancellation date of between 60 and 90 days, as in, if the books don't arrive by a certain date, the order is cancelled. Period.

Selling Rights
and Permissions

MOST AUTHORS WANT TO SEE AN EXCERPT of their book in Cosmopolitan, Time, Vanity Fair and so on. How do you get it into any of these publications? Let's talk about foreign rights first.

All languages, except for your own, won't happen until an English version is available first. Reason: they have to estimate how much it would cost to translate, whether they should copy the original style and format, etc. Usually the rule of thumb is if the publication is going to print 5000 copies, and sell for the equivalent of 20$ US each, you would be advanced 25—50% of potential revenue. For example, if the royalty rate is 5% on the first print run, you'd be getting .50 / book x 2500 books equals your advance payment, usually payable in three steps: ⅓ signing, ⅓ publication, and ⅓ 60 days after.

What are the chances of selling to foreign markets? If it's a self-help, business or a general non-fiction book that is not regional in nature, foreign sales are feasible. Travel and children's books do well also; so, you have a reasonable chance— assuming you are working through an international literary agent. There are several ways of accomplishing this. You can use your distributor to approach the international marketplace on your behalf; you can go to international rights agencies.

There are also Rights fairs that take place around the world. The biggest one is the Frankfurt fair, second week in October. Book Expo America is held in the late Spring, which can be anywhere in the US (Chicago, NY or LA are the most likely venues). Self-publishers can register as individuals or as publishers; the cost is about $150 US.

For selling Translation rights into the French language in Canada, look for Salon de Livres, held in Montreal in late October.

Virtually every country in the world has a Rights fair.

Frankfurt is the only one that is truly international and virtually every country attends; the London Book Fair is close behind in early Spring, with Book Expo America rapidly gaining ground.

Please note that the odds are 99% against a publisher making a commitment during a book fair. You are making contacts, getting promises to send the book and you can expect a response within about 2 or 3 months with an offer—if there is interest.

To find Rights agents, check out Bowker International Literary Book Marketplace, as some agents list their subject areas.

With respect to Spanish language rights, this is the fastest growing language rights market, primarily for education and reference materials. Foreign language rights are normally granted on a world-wide basis.

The only language that isn't broken down by territory or continent, is the /English language.

TV/Movie/Film

Get a lawyer.

Other Sales Opportunities

Corporate Sales

These sales are directed at the Human Resources Director, President, or Executive VP of Sales. These are the people who are passionately interested in doing their jobs well.

99.9% of commercial distributors do not do corporate sales: you are relying on your own efforts. There are companies that specialize in these types of sales, and they are paid an upfront retainer or a monthly retainer. So, unless you have $5,000 to burn, do it yourself. It's very similar to PR: you can hire someone to do these things and they may have the contacts, but you're probably better off doing this sort of thing yourself.

Motivational speakers books have a good chance of being sold because you're speaking to these people anyway.

Don't be surprised if you're asked to make some editorial changes, redesign cover, and so on to make changes. If you get an order for 25,000 books, these changes are not a problem.

Seminar Sales

Let's say you've written a book on car care, the best way to sell your books is to approach a local car dealer or parts store and organize a seminar. You have to create your own publicity material and perhaps give them a percentage of book sales, but the point is you need to create your own selling opportunities and they will be a lot easier to execute than you may think.

Last Words

ISHOULD PROBABLY HAVE STARTED *The Insiders Guide to Self-Publishing* with these last words because they're a little kinder. In truth, I think the only things that I'm more proud of than being an author is being the father of my two boys and new daughter. Honestly, there are uncanny similarities between a book and a child. What the hell am I talking about? Think about it. Both require an effort to produce and deliver. Both need constant nurturing, attention and money. And regardless of how you feel about your book or child on any given day, you can't give up on either, or the unthinkable will happen: they'll die. I know it's dramatic, but it's true. Your book, your pride and joy, the consumer of so much of your time and effort, will live or die at your hands.

Now's a good time to give you an industry snapshot, an idea of where publishing is headed, according to the insiders. There are good things happening in this industry after a number of years dominated by fairly negative things. For the self-published author, here are the things worth knowing:

1. children's book titles are up 25% in 2003 over the previous year [they've since taken a downturn because it seems TV shows like Barney have finally taken their toll on young readers' attention spans]
2. overall titles are up 19%
3. self-published growth categories include:

   a. religious titles
   b. self-help books
   c. children's books
   d. brand name series
   e. non-fiction

In truth, there are very few moments as meaningful in your life as the first time you hold your freshly printed book. Only a mother, probably, can have experienced something akin to the sensation of holding something you've thought about, fretted over, nurtured and labored over for untold months. Done right, your book will be a defining moment in your life. If you're a speaker, your fees will go up 50% because of you having a book. Speaking personally, my book, Cook Like a Mother! Clean Like a Pro! opened the doors to teaching a cooking class for the domestically challenged and opened up sponsorship relationships and speaking avenues previously unavailable. That's on my humble level.

Of course, done wrong, there are very few things that will be as absolute a consumer of time and money as publishing a book.

And to that point, you have to hope you'll be exposed to as many good-hearted, honest people as I was when I was completely clueless starting out (I'm still clueless but I've graduated from completely to just selectively clueless). You have to hope you'll have an honest distributor who will pay you, first of all, and secondly, give you the time of day on matters of importance to you but of things they've gone through a thousand times before, and only the kind ones will take the time to explain it just one more time.

And finally, after all my caveats and negativisms, I truly hope you fulfill your dream of being a published author!

Bill has the following caution: as a first time author, you naturally expect the world to come knocking at your door, and unfortunately, it just won't happen. You have to knock on the world's door. Major newspapers, magazines and electronic media will probably not review your book, unless you have wonderful advance quotes. By wonderful, he's referring to a quote from someone like Bill Clinton or Oprah, or leading authorities in the field.

Start your media campaign where you live, as they will most likely want to support a local author. Local newspapers, radio and TV stations are mandated to support local initiatives and you can benefit from this. Be sure to have tapes of everything you do on TV and radio to send to other markets. You can either record these shows yourself or ask a few of your friends and family to do so in case your recording messes up. You can't always rely on the TV stations to provide you with a copy.

Always remember that as a self-published author you have one great advantage: you will still be promoting your book this selling season, the next selling season and the season after that, whereas for the most part, if it was conventionally published as a Spring or Fall title (a publishing house), they will have moved on to the next season's offerings.

Good luck and much success on your journey!